Echoes Of An Unfinished Soul

20 Something & The Lost In Between

Kienna Rodriguez

BookLeaf Publishing

India | USA | UK

Made with ❤ on the BookLeaf Publishing Platform
www.bookleafpub.in
www.bookleafpub.com

Dedication

To the twenty-somethings, the wanderers in the space between youth and adulthood- this is for you. For those who find themselves caught in the strange limbo of becoming, where the world feels both vast and suffocating. Growing up is not a destination but a constant unfolding, full of questions and contradictions, doubts and revelations. The journey can be disorienting, but it is also where the echoes of our past meet the hopes of our future.

May this be a reminder that even in the uncertainty, there is a power in your becoming. You are not lost, but in the process of finding your own rhythm. In the quiet spaces between expectations and reality, let your soul be both a question and an answer. Trust that each step forward, no matter how unsure, carries the promise of transformation.

May this book be a celebration of that journey- the messy, the beautiful, and everything in between. You are allowed to be unfinished, but within that, you are already whole.

Preface

The twenties are an odd and enigmatic decade, a strange blend of freedom and uncertainty, of old identities shedding and new ones struggling to root. It's a time when you're expected to have it all figured out, yet more often than not, you find yourself questioning who you are, where you're going, and what it all means. The world tells you to grow up, to step into your purpose, to carve out a place for yourself- but the truth is, the road to adulthood is rarely linear, and the answers are often elusive.

This book, *Echoes of an Unfinished Soul,* is an exploration of that tension, that beautiful, messy space where we find ourselves standing between the past and the future, between childhood dreams and adult realities. It is a reflection on the struggle to define ourselves in a world that constantly shifts beneath our feet, and the quiet wisdom that emerges from allowing ourselves to be both lost and found in the same breath.

Through philosophy, introspection, and a touch of manifestation, this collection of thoughts, reflections, and musings seek to hold space for those in the liminal moments of life. For those who feel the pull to grow, to change, but still feel tethered to the versions of themselves they are outgrowing. For those who find solace in the unknown, and those who dream of something more but can't quite see it yet.

This is not a book with answers. It is an invitation- a call to embrace the unfinished, the fragmented, the evolving nature of self. The twenties are not a time to be rushed through or neatly defined; they are a time to lean into the paradox, to find meaning in the mess. In the pages that follow, I hope you'll find a sense of companionship and affirmation, knowing that if you're in this strange, liminal space, you're exactly where you need to be. The journey is unfolding, and it is full of possibility.

Welcome to the in-between. May you discover that even in the uncertainty, you are already becoming.

Acknowledgements

To my family, whose unwavering support has been a constant thread throughout this journey. Your love and belief in me, even when I couldn't quite believe in myself, has been the foundation of everything I've written here.

To my love and my friends, who have stood by me through the highs and lows of this strange decade. Thank you for the late night talks, the moments of laughter, and constant inspiration. You are my mirrors and anchors in this chaotic world.

To those who have walked with me through the transition from youth to adulthood, each conversation, each experience, has shaped this work. This book is as much yours as it is mine. The wisdom shared and the lessons learned have all been a part of this process.

To the universe, for always providing exactly what I need, even when I don't know it yet. In the moments of doubt and uncertainty, you've guided me to the answers that live within, even when they're hidden in plain sight. Thank you for the gentle nudges and the quiet reminders to trust the process.

Finally, to every twenty-something out there- lost, confused, hopeful, or just trying to figure it out. This is for you. If you ever feel adrift in the vastness of this world, know that this book is a reflection of that very feeling. May it remind you that even in the unknown, you are exactly where you need to be, and you are becoming something beautiful. Thank you for walking this journey with me.

1. past, present, future

Past, present future.

I endeavor to live in one, yet I live in two I cannot infiltrate.

Past, future.

Present.

The present is a gift I do not open until it is too late.

It's as if Christmas Day has come to an end.

The lights glimmer across the windows, and the gift of presence is wrapped and unopened by the tree.

If I was given the present as a gift at white elpehant, I would steal another gift.

I DON'T WANT IT.

I reflect on my present as if it is already behind me.

I live in the present as if I am not coexisting with it.

Someone else can have this moment, I want the future.

I want to lay softly on my deathbed knowing I accomplished everything I was destined for.

Only the future holds that gift.

The present tells me I am on my way, I am on the right path.

The future is the path already paved, discovered, understood.

The present is navigation.

It's the consant U-turns to bad habits and poor communication.

I want to be the best woman I can become, only the future knows who that woman is.

The present is unpaved, unknown, undecided.

The present is the journey, the future is the destination.

2. insecurities

A stretch mark, breast size, the color of your hair.

The words being said.

The insecurities we carry.

Sting like the rage of an irritated bee.

Follow like the path of the water.

Can never escape the expectations of our mirror.

The curve of your lips or your hips.

Hug your body tightly.

Your skull nurtures your beauty.

You do not.

3. perfection haunts

Scales.

The scale only widens.

The fear of imperfection is not hollow.

Weight.

Grades.

Credit.

Perfection haunts.

4. gifted

The gift.

Flesh

Skin

Bones

Your curves are blessed

The body

You're given

Is designed

For you

ONLY.

5. wendy

I used to believe dreams were for princesses in movies and girls in their little worlds.

I was that girl stuck in that little world.

I used to pray I would stay seven for another ten years;

That I would become Wendy from Peter Pan while I cried for the fear of growing boobs or liking boys.

I am no longer Wendy from Peter Pan.

In fact, I don't believe I ever was.

I just wanted to believe I was, so I could stay in that little world.

I am now a twenty two year old girl with big dreams in a big world with every possibility of making it or not.

I stare at computer screens, praying I will get a scholarship or sign a record deal after sending one small email.

It's a big email in my little, self involved, teenage brain.

I grew from juice boxes to milkshakes because deep down, I am still a seven year old waiting to become Wendy from Peter Pan.

I can't drive nor get a job because of these facts of my little girl life.

I write poems for people who may possibly understand my feelings or ignore them all together.

I try to find beauty in every tadpole or sunset and find myself smiling from the numbness of teenage life issues; Such as friends glaring at you from across the gym or getting a B- in US History.

I slab expensive products of makeup on my face not for the fact of feeling better about myself, but to feel just as cool as others look when they talk to me and I am wearing my mother's sweatpants with yesterday night's greasy, messy bun.

But throughout the twenty-two years of convincing myself not to grow up, I did learn a few things while whining about how uncomfortable bras are.

I learned that you mold yourself into who you want to
be understood as and you make yourself something in
this world.

You stay up until midnight memorizing Italian diction
not to learn Italian, but to learn the art form that is called
music.

You paint a room not for the look, but for how it makes
you feel.

You paint your wrinkled, tired eyes with expensive
powders not to look pretty, but to make art.

You make the world what you want to see by forcing the
world to see your art.

I still believe that dreams are for princesses in movies
and little girls in their little worlds.

But my little world will always be my expression of my
art.

6. messy

Love is messy.

Love is an unkind volcano waiting to erupt

Love is powerful and unwelcoming

My love is yours.

It is messy and unkind; but it is yours

You shall take it with two hands turning to fists

It will erupt in your palms and overflow into a puddle of red

My love is overpowering

It is bright and bold

But it is true.

7. letters to self - 2023

2023 was kind, and it was harsh.

Kienna flourished, Kienna failed.

She thrived and loved herself as well as others, but she also had days where she couldn't stand being in her own skin.

She couldn't escape her negative thoughts or the dismissive people she was surrounded by.

She couldn't grow into who she was because her path had ended where she thought it began.

Kienna kept expecting things to improve, and to feel included, cherished and loved.

2023 was a whirlwind of emotions and changes that SHE made for ME.

As I celebrate the end of 2023, I celebrate life for Kienna.

This year, I saw four countries, got my limit of tattoos for the year, made new friends, and lost too many friends to count.

 I spent too much money, found love, and found my passions.

I accepted my first big girl job and am one step closer to receiving a degree.

2023 was kind, and it was harsh.

Kienna flourished, Kienna failed.

I am proud of Kienna.

8. liberation

Each moment is pregnant with liberation.

The only way illusions work is if I mistake it for reality.

I see the awakened quality in me.

I decide what I align myself with.

Each moment is pregnant with liberation.

I will grasp it.

9. being

The molding.

Your brain.

Your eyes.

Your fingertips.

Your mold is thrown away as you are born.

The being called "you"

Irreplaceable.

10. africa

The Kienna I know did not come to Africa, she was left behind in the States.

But when she did visit Africa, she became the dust that blows through the desert,

Creating a symphony of sand with the wind.

Swirling and twirling around the dead branches of the singing trees.

She ran with the lions and grazed with the zebras.

She became whole in a place she never knew she needed.

11. don't be political

No one will ever silence me, gaslight me, or take away my power that lives deep within my soul.

No one will ever take away my greatness, ability to succeed, or my fire to fight for a democracy that we desperately need to see flourish.

I refuse to let anyone strip the rights of those I love, and those I have yet to love.

You deserve to thrive and retain your human and civil rights.

Knowledge is readily available for you to prepare to take over the world.

And we'll all do it together.

12. she

The path I have taken has hurt me beyond the ways I can put into words, but it has made me a passionate friend, daughter, and artist.

 I am thankful for the bruises and scars I have from getting my heart broken for the first time or scraping my knee tripping in the arroyo.

Where I have grown up to the people I have been friends with, they have vanished like the adolescence I once carried.

I am now an adult and still reach and pull for the young child I knew.

I was.

She is within me and she always will be. She is channeled, she is present.

She is me.

13. take a second glance

It has taken my whole twenty-two years of living, breathing and growing to understand who I truly am while there is still so much more to discover.

 I am straightforward and sometimes, pushy.

I am messy and hide my messes behind my bed to avoid the issue I will someday confront.

My room is extremely organized from a first glance, but look at something for a few moments too long and you will catch a glimpse of broken cracks and dirt hidden behind the surface.

I am childish and loud; speeding through the aisles of target on a skateboard I am convincing myself I know how to ride.

I am hardworking and devoted when I truly force myself to sit down and view a new opportunity.

I am brave and obnoxious in the times I should really just sit quietly.

I am nosy and naive, but it is who I was made to be.

I have learned over the twenty-two years of living, breathing and growing, that I am worth so much more than a first glance.

14. fears

Fear of spiders in my shower, fear of heights. Once when I was in sixth grade, my class took a trip to the Santa Fe Community College to go ziplining. Fear of vocal nodules; fear of waking up during surgery: fear of contacts, eyes overall actually. Fear that I will forget all the lines to a show I am in and stand on stage awkwardly waiting to remember what to do. Fear of slenderman or any tall creature with no face. Once, when I was about twelve, my cousin was living with me and she would constantly tell me stories of slenderman and finish it off by saying "Walk safe to the bus tomorrow. Don't let slenderman get you." She would shut off the light and I'd lay in terror. Things like that show how gullible I used to be.

Fear of getting struck by lightning, fear of snakes, fear of drivers in New Mexico, fear of the guilt I build up in my mind. Once, I was throwing a ball around my room and broke my hello kitty clock into shattered pieces; when my mom asked who did it, I blamed my overly large cat Christopher. Fear of surprises. Fear of unexpected visits to the hospital. Fear of being lost in the woods, fear of my old hunting horse Sally who could not walk in water or ice for the life of her. Fear of cops even when they are not there for me; fear of long responses to short questions; fear of teachers giving me bad grades for something I turned in. Fear that I may not graduate college or even highschool.

When I was younger and learning how to ride a horse, my father was teaching me how to turn him around. I turned too hard and the reins pulled tight against his neck. My horse ran two houses down my road while I held onto the horn releasing the reins. He stopped at the corrals down the road to greet the other horses. My neighbors laughed while I cried.

Once, I was afraid of Woody from "Toy Story" but that was when I was three and he was nothing compared to Stitch or Barney. Once in fifth grade, we were making oobleck for our science class and the texture made my best friend cry whenever she held it. I liked it. Especially how it dried on my fingers and I could rub it off. Later, we were swimming in a lake and she felt a fish brush against her leg. She had a panic attack and my parents and I took her home. Now, we don't talk.

People go backpacking alone for months throughout the United States and even the world. I am not afraid of being alone. I am afraid of being stuck with one person for a long period of time with no escape.

Cats can sleep up to 18 hours a day. I have more energy when I don't sleep as many hours as I should.
My cat Sinatra likes to chase dogs but is afraid of my fish. I am afraid he will become scared of everything smaller than him.

Once, I was practicing for an archery tournament and saw a bobcat cub standing behind my target. Once I saw a flock of geese flying over while I was sledding. Once I watched my cat eat a lizard's head.

I may have lots of fears; but standing here now, I know I belong.

15. faith

I've never been very spiritually attached.
I have always relied on myself to get out of harsh
situations. But there was one special day where I needed
guidance. My father was off in town drinking countless
beers in some dirt patch with buddies throwing
horseshoes and my mother was only God knows where.
It was the time in my life where I was constantly
vulnerable and alone. I had no hope.

The mountain behind my house was steep and
overgrown with trees surrounded by barbed wire. Rocks
piled at the top of the skinny mountain. They stumbled
on top of each other and occasionally traveled down the
hill. Wedged in between those large rocks, was a cross.
My grandfather's cross. His ashes hidden below the
rocks rising up through the wood.

That day when my parents had left me to be
hopeless at home, I found my hope on that mountain. On
those rocks and next to that cross, I saw a new world of
faith. I saw the change I needed in my life.

I climbed up the steep mountain slipping through
loose dirt and digging my palms into the jagged barbed

wire fence. As I climbed, the sun beamed through that cross. It blinded me, but my heart thumped. I felt him. He was with me, and so was God. I grasped the rough edge of the rocks and pulled myself up next to that cross. I felt the wind, and in that wind was a powerful feeling of love.

I wasn't alone.

I was never alone.

I was with him.

16. inside my brain

Inside my brain there is a small girl in the corner.

She wails and cries and fears for herself in this big terrifying world.

She fears for her loved ones and those she has yet to know.

She fears for the mothers and children of the world and prays every father is better, or at least as good as her own.

She curses those who believe in religious persecution and subjecting women to violence.

She hopes for the brighter future she sees and manifests in her mind.

She wants the world to love each and every individual as much as she loves herself.

She wishes the best upon everyone she greets and everyone she meets.

Yet it never feels like enough.

17. what of my safety?

When I was young, about middle school, so eleven or twelve.

I had a choir teacher who hated movement while we performed.

It was his biggest annoyance and my biggest fear.

Any itch, scratch or reaction had to be held in, hidden from any eyes or souls.

Especially Mr. Prenevost's.

If we disrupted the fluidity, how the song interwines and nuzzles inside itself.

How *we* did that to the music.

Our voices the vessel.

Our bodies the anchor.

How the music wanes and cries out to be heard.

To be known.

How each note caresses the next, slowly evolving into another.

There was a performance where a girl looked to the girl standing next to hear and giggled.

Mr. Prenevost stopped the entire performance.

He yelled at the top of his lungs while an audience of parents and siblings gawked at the sight to see.

He made her publicly apologize to the audience and started the song over again.

Tears filled her eyes and her face flushed with shades of red.

I was filled with anxiety and fear.

You never protected me from those feelings.

You instilled them in me.

You put those situations in my lap like fireworks on my eyelashes.

An overwhelming feeling and shrieks as the light bursts in the sky.

Children filled with adrenaline and fear and excitement.

But you stay away from fireworks from your safety, running far away from harm.

What of my safety?

Nine-year-old Kienna yearns to be safe.

She sat in the passenger seat at a young age fearing for her life with your hands at the wheel.

Your mind distracted by rage and desire to show people who is right.

It was never me.

18. time

I walk past the classroom we used to share.

If I knew then what I know now, maybe I would have cherished those moments more.

If I could sit in that moment, I would smile.

I would doubt you.

I wouldn't know you.

We were just kids.

I thought I knew me, knew you, knew her.

Knew us.

Time wasn't our friend and I'm not mad at it.

You are who you were meant to be and I accept you in your true form.

You are still goodness and grace.

I just now recently learned that you could be replaced.

If I could sit in that moment, maybe I would smile.

But since then, I have grown a good while.

Time wasn't our friend, but it has always been kind.

I'm thankful for what we had, but I am more grateful for time.

19. letters to self- 2024

Welcome to a new year and a new story to tell.

You have been extremely hard on yourself this year but you have also taken great strides as the woman that you are now becoming.

You met the happiest and saddest versions of yourself this year, yet you both took pride in each side.

I am in love with every piece and part of you, and I promise to always walk by your side with love, positivity, and faith.

You have grown immensely in the last year.

You have found successes in unforeseen places.

You will continue to only gravitate towards peace and graciousness and satiate the foundation you are building.

Never lose hope or trust in yourself or the universe.

You got this.

20. aging

Time is not my friend.

I thought it was, until I looked in the mirror and I no longer the sixteen-year-old girl who was learning the world from a clear scope.

My lens is muddied, unclear and quite frankly, confusing.

I went from a senior in highschool auditioning for prestigious liberal arts schools to a senior in college with a pre-law degree.

Time is not my friend.

August of 2023, I saw the first wrinkle on my forehead and felt like time flew twenty years into the future.

I envisioned I had become acquaintances with my forty-year-old self.

I didn't want to see her. I never want to see her again.

My grandmother has cursed her aging since the age of coherence.

Our phone calls always start with her aches and pains, how they are the same as the day before.

Dull, but visible.

Painful, but not anything she hasn't endured before.

I refuse to take my youth for granted yet, I can't wait to have stability.

I refuse to let my craziness go to waste yet, I am persistent in being poised and polite.

My maturity stole my youth.

My question is how do we contain our youth and prepare to meet death at any moment?

Time is not my friend.

My junior year of college, I became a primary caregiver.

My junior year of college, I grasped aging.

It took me in a chokehold and made me accept my inevitable fate of aging.

I thought aging was a gift, until my grandmother could
no longer leave the house.

I drive her to medical appointments and fear when she
enters those doors, she will not exit.

Everytime, she returns to me.

She *returns*.

For that, time is my friend.

www.ingramcontent.com/pod-product-compliance
Lightning Source LLC
LaVergne TN
LVHW010914200726

843509LV00013B/1932